MW00915182

STOP TEST ANXIETY

Test-taking Strategies that Use the Power of Your Subconscious Mind

By Dr. Wanita Holmes

This book will help you eliminate old thoughts that hold you back. It will work best when used with the companion hypnosis MP3's available for purchase at:

holmeshypnotherapy.com/mp3s

It's time to end text anxiety and take tests without fear of failure...

TABLE OF CONTENTS

CHAPTER 8: VISUALIZE YOURSELF ON TEST DAY

WHY DID I WRITE THIS BOOK?

I wrote this book because of my clients' success in overcoming test anxiety and their ability to feel good about themselves and to pass tests even after failing many times.

I realized I could only work with so many people one-on-one in my office. However I always wanted to help many more people. The obvious answer was to write a book. I decided I would write this book as though you were actually in my office and we were working together.

When I first see my new client, I work with them to build their confidence, develop self esteem, get rid of fears, anxiety, negativity, and self-defeating thoughts. I then teach them step by easy step, how to study. After that we then work on how to take a test. And then I do a hypnosis session to educate their subconscious mind how to relax, how to study, and how to take tests.

All of this information is in this book and is reinforced with the hypnotherapy MP3's that I have created to accompany and enhance the results.

Enjoy your new experience of learning!

ABOUT THE STOP TEST ANXIETY MP3'S

This book contains all that you need to know about studying and test-taking. However, the two companion hypnosis MP3's I have created to accompany this book will amplify and accelerate your learning. They are *Stop Test Anxiety #1 How to Study* and *Stop Test Anxiety #2 Stop Test Anxiety*.

The first MP3, *How to Study*, will reinforce all of the methods this book will teach you to improve your ability to study and retain the material you need to learn.

The second MP3, *Stop Test Anxiety*, will program your subconscious mind to relax and do your best on test day.

As you listen every night, your subconscious mind will be infused with powerful thoughts that will quickly eradicate all the accumulated negativity and replace those old, fearful, negative stories with confidence in your ability to take tests and to pass.

Attention: Do not listen to your MP3's while driving or operating any moving vehicle or equipment that requires your full attention.

Always put a light cover over yourself because as your brainwaves slow down, you may get cooler. It is difficult to relax or drift off to sleep when you are cold. It is recommended that you listen to your MP3's every night for at least three weeks as you drift off to sleep. This is passive reinforcement that will enable you to retain all you have studied, and be relaxed and excited to take your next test.

As an added bonus you will sleep deep, restful sleep and awaken in the morning refreshed and ready for your new day.

Instant downloads of the *How to Study* and *Stop Test Anxiety* MP3's are available for a nominal price here:

holmeshypnotherapy.com/mp3s

INTRODUCTION

This book and companion hypnosis MP3's are filled with empowering information. This is all you need to begin making the changes that will enable you to live up to your full potential.

It has taken me many years and over 40,000 sessions with clients, listening to people relate their fears, their frustrations, their life disappointments, and their unfulfilled dreams and quiet desperation, for me to put it all together. I've come to the conclusion that getting rid of your problem is not that complicated or difficult.

Many people treat their challenges as though they were a calculus problem when their problem is as simple as 1+1=2!

Really?

Yes!

You are a body and thoughts. Your thoughts create your behavior. When you choose to change a behavior, you must change the thoughts behind the behavior.

Then with practice, the behavior will change automatically.

Simple and amazing, isn't it?

Interestingly, over 2000 years ago, someone knew that this was so. They knew then what this book will be teaching you now:

"In the beginning there was the Word... and the word became the flesh."

And consider these wise words:

"Whatsoever you think, so shall you become. If you think yourself weak, weak you will be. If you think yourself strong, strong you will be."

~ Swami Vivekananda 1863- 1902

Do you get it?

1+1=2.

You become what you think!

Listen, you do not have to spend years and 1000s of dollars rehashing your problem in order to change. This is not rocket science! All you need to know is that you are truly what you think.

Get rid of old, negative stories. Create new, power-ful, self-affirming stories. That's it! Change your stories, change your life!

This book and companion MP3's will teach you how to do this. Be ready and willing to do the work. Read and re-read this book. Listen to your MP3'S for 21 days.

Monitor your thoughts.

Change those stumbling blocks into stepping-stones!

March on!

Get ready.

Get set.

Go!

About Your Book

This book is divided into three sections.

Section 1: It's All About You

Stop kidding yourself. Now is the time to have fun. Let go of all the test and studying anxieties. No more excuses; no more bad habits; no more broken promises to yourself. Section 1 enables you to let go of all that has held you back and show you how to recognize your potential. And the best part is, how to go for it.

Section 2: A New Way to Study

A sure-fire new way to study. You will look forward to studying. No kidding. No more resistance. No more procrastinating. Trust me, you will look forward to studying, starting now! Today! Because tomorrow never comes!

Section 3: A New Way to Take a Test

Bravo! You've come this far and now it's almost test time. Section 3 will prepare you for test day. You've done your part. You are ready, you are motivated, and you will now learn how to use all that you have learned.

Relax.

You're on your way.

SECTION 1:
IT'S ALL ABOUT YOU

CHAPTER 1:
EMPOWER YOURSELF

TAKE THE FIRST STEP

Ask yourself, "Why did I buy this book?"

Is it because you, like so many others, don't have a clue about how to study?

Are you terrified when it comes to taking tests and exams?

Are you someone who is unable to remember what you have read or studied?

Do you sweat or hyperventilate just thinking about an upcoming exam or even just reading about it?

If you do, then this book is for you. It is exactly what you need.

I don't care if you have flunked tests in the past. I don't care if you dread sitting down and studying. I don't care if you are in grade school, high school, college, law school, medical school, or any other school.

None of that matters.

What does matter, and what I care about, is helping you get rid of your negative programming.

What does matter is for you to have an open mind and a willingness to do the work.

All you have to do is read and follow the instructions in this book and listen to the companion MP3's for 21 days.

Now I ask you, how hard is that?

At first it may seem hard. You may think there's too much to learn. Don't let that thought take hold in your brain! Very soon, sooner than you think, you will discover you can do it, easily and effortlessly.

How great is that?

INTENTIONS

Every day from this day forward, practice starting your day with powerful intentions. The way you start your day will be how your day will play out.

You are reading this book because you have the intention to change the way that you study and how to pass your exams.

Changing a behavior can feel like a huge challenge. Many of you want to change but are afraid to get out of the rut that you are in, the rut with which you are so familiar.

Perhaps you are not sure how to behave as you begin to be the successful person you choose to be. Sometimes failure becomes the focal point of your identity. Who would you be without that crutch?

Remember you have to go out on the limb to get the sweetest fruit! You can always continue to cling to the safety of the trunk of the tree of life but if you want the sweetest fruit, you have to let go of the trunk and climb out on the limb.

Oh! You're afraid the limb might break? You are right! It might. If it breaks, you will fall down. So what? Pick yourself up, dust yourself off, and start all over again!

Don't be afraid to get out of your rut. Just have the courage to let go of the safety of the tree trunk.

Be filled with the power of your intentions.

Declare who you want to be.

Demand to be your best.

You deserve it.

Go for it!

MOTIVATION

The next thing you need to think about is: what do you really want? Don't just read this and pass over it. You must know what you want.

What do you want?

How are you going to get it?

When do you want to get it?

What are you willing to do to get it?

And, what will you do when you do get it?

Any goal you have needs to have an end result in order for you to achieve it. If you can't picture your end result, you are just spinning your wheels and going nowhere.

So... from this day forward, see yourself taking tests relaxed, at ease, and passing those tests. And re-member - you don't need to be perfect, you just have to pass.

You have probably heard that what your mind can conceive, you can achieve. This simple thought probably went in one ear and out the other. Listen! Your subconscious mind does not know the difference between fantasy and reality, so always see yourself in the most positive way.

Today, you are going to believe it! You are going to be motivated to commit to it, and you will use it to serve you every day.

You were motivated to buy this book and you did! You are committed to do the work and you will! You are disciplined to do whatever you need to do to and you will!

You will learn new ways to study and you will pass your exams easily and effortlessly.

You can do it.

You will do it.

You are going to do it.

Chapter 2:
Change Your Mindset

No More Excuses

Starting now, you will never underestimate your potential. You are pure potential. Never again make excuses regarding your abilities, your talents, your creativity, your power, your intelligence, your ability to study, memorize, retain information, and to pass tests.

Listen, if you don't toot your own horn, you ain't never going to hear the music! Don't wait for someone else to do it. You do it! It is not conceit; it is simply a willingness to acknowledge your own worth.

The world is a mirror; it reflects back what you think about yourself.

Recently I received a call from a lady in Phoenix, Arizona. She had just completed her training to be a hypnotherapist. She said she had heard about me and wondered if I could give her some advice to help her get her practice started.

As I listened to her, she uttered one excuse after another about why she had not yet started to practice. She didn't have a computer. She didn't have the right phone. Didn't know how to get clients. Couldn't afford an office. And she had no business cards. Excuses, excuses, excuses.

I suggested that she start going to local chamber meetings, Women In Business meetings, networking meetings. I urged her to get business cards immediately and to always include her card with the tip she leaves when at a restaurant. I told her to ask people what they do so they would then ask her what she did.

However, before she got off the phone she said, "I would like to thank you for your time Dr. Wanita, but you don't understand how it is here. It's really very hot here in Phoenix and people just don't want to leave their air-conditioned houses."

Say what? I was born in Phoenix! I know how hot it is. P.S. Everything is air-conditioned.

So what's your excuse? How many excuses do you have that are holding you back? What is keeping you from tooting your own horn and hearing your own music?

Think about it.

Start playing your own music today.

HIGH EXPECTATIONS

High expectations require that you must show up. That's right! Every day you must allot time to study. Every day you must be committed to exercise your brain just as you would take time to exercise your body.

Every day demand the best for yourself. This requires that you pay attention to your old negative dialogue. Stop it! Change it!

Remember your subconscious mind doesn't know the difference between fantasy and reality.

Surprise!

It does what you tell it to do. Your conscious mind thinks the thought and your subconscious mind acts it out.

If you tell yourself you're terrified to take tests, you will be terrified. If you think you will fail, you will fail.

The conscious mind thinks the thought; the subconscious mind acts it out. Get it? Therefore why not think positive thoughts? Just tell your subconscious mind, "I used to be afraid to take tests. I choose not to be that way anymore. I look forward to studying and passing my tests. I can do it."

People who are successful have high expectations. They think strong and powerful thoughts. They expect their dreams to happen. They understand how thoughts work for them.

It's not magic. It just feels like it.

Remember, you must show up. Do the work. Pay attention to your thoughts. Have high expectations for yourself. Expect success. Change your thoughts. Change your reality.

Sound easy?

It is!

Just do it!

SELF CONFIDENCE/SELF ESTEEM

As you read this book and listen to your MP3's, you will be changing the way you think about test anxiety and studying

In the past you have stored in your mind all the negative stories and negative thought forms that have held you back. For just a moment, think about all the crap that has kept you from moving forward and achieving your goals.

Now, in a moment I want you to close your eyes and take a deep relaxing breath and then exhale very slowly and as you do, think of all the powerful positive qualities you already have and the new ones you want to have.

Come on. Just do it. Close your eyes, breathe, and imagine you have an eraser. Use it to erase all those negative stories from the blackboard of your mind. Stories that have held you back. Tell yourself "These stories have no meaning for me anymore. None at all."

Change your story. See, sense and feel yourself very confident, very certain of your new ability to study and to pass your test. Hear your inner voice say, "I can do it. I am capable and intelligent. I choose to no longer indulge in negative thoughts, feelings, or actions."

You now choose not to be a victim of your negative thinking.

You are confident.

You have elevated your self-esteem.

You get it.

These are the keys to your success.

Chapter 3:
Prepare for Change

What Would You Like to Have Happen?

Most likely, you bought this book because you want to learn a new way to study, a new way to pass tests and exams.

The first thing I want you to do now is get a pen or pencil and some paper.

Do not continue reading! Stop for a moment and get up and get some paper and something to write with.

When you're ready, you're going to write down your answers to the following questions. Take your time and be honest.

1. Why did you buy this book?

2. What do you hope to get from this book?

3. What school do you attend or plan to attend?

4. How are your grades in school?

5. Do you hate or enjoy school?

6. How do you usually do on tests?

7. How are your study habits?

8. What is the most difficult thing about studying?

9. Where do you usually study?

10. What time of day do you usually study?

11. How much time do you study each day?

12. What bothers you most about taking tests?

13. Write down anything you can think of that gets in the way of you doing your best.

Don't despair. In Section Two of this book I'm going to teach you the secrets of exactly how to study and how to let go of any negativity connected with test-taking. Learning new ways to study will enable you to let go of the fear of test-taking.

Don't believe me?

Remember $1+1=2$.

Read on!

ASPIRE HIGHER

One of the most important changes that you will make is this: From now on, choose to surround yourself with people and other students who are smart and successful. Don't settle to be king or queen of the dung heap!

Choose to keep company with winners, people who are positive and upbeat, people who will lift you up, who will encourage you, stimulate you and get you thinking in the most positive ways.

This does not mean that you should look down on other people who are struggling or down on their luck. However, for you to change, you need to associate with people who do get it, people who do the work and achieve their goals.

Their positive attitudes will rub off on you, just as negative attitudes will rub off on you!

Which will you choose? You always have a choice about how you fill your life.

You can choose to soar with the eagles or you can choose to commiserate with failures.

What do you choose?

Take your pick.

WILLINGNESS

This book requires that you have a willingness to do the work. Don't just breeze through it. Instead read out loud, underline, highlight, dog-ear, and make notes.

Take it all in and then re-read. Share what you have learned with other positive people. Get excited!

As you do the work, you will be learning new, simple ways to improve your studying. This will enable you to feel confident that you can and will pass any test you prepare for.

Remember, it's not magic. You must be willing to do the work. Willingness is a state of mind. Just be willing. Do the work. Only then will it feel magical. So...

Practice, practice, practice!

CHAPTER 4:
HOW TO RETRAIN YOUR BRAIN

BE CLEAR

Why are you pursuing a particular career? Is it your dream, your desire, your passion? Or is it because your family insists that you "should" be a teacher, a doctor, a lawyer, a policeman, or a computer geek? Perhaps it just "runs in your family" and that led to your decision.

Take the time now to, once again, get a paper and something to write with. Write down all the reasons that led you to decide to go into law, medicine, or?

Take your time. Come on! Do it!

I once worked with a client who had failed the Bar Exam four times. During our work he revealed to me that he had only gone to law school because his family insisted on it. He hated law! He took the exam the fifth time and he failed again. (By the way that was the only time I also failed!)

He got it. I got it. His family finally got it. He quit trying to pass the Bar Exam and became a successful building contractor instead.

Quite the opposite was a lady who failed to pass the Bar Exam twice. Unwittingly, her mother was part of the problem. Each time my client prepared to take the exam, her mother would console her and say, "Don't worry dear. If you fail again, you can always be a paralegal."

What a stumbling block she created for her daughter. After working with her on how to study, how to regain her confidence, and how to take the exam, she passed! She currently works in Sacramento as an advocate for women's legal issues.

Do what you have a passion for!

Power Your Brain

You are about to learn new ways to improve your study habits. Now you understand that you have a thinking mind (your conscious mind) and an action mind (your subconscious mind). Your subconscious mind is always open and ready to carry out your instructions.

Remember, your conscious mind thinks the thought; your subconscious mind acts it out.

So whatever you tell your subconscious mind to do, it does it. Even if it's a lie. It is rather like your computer: "Garbage in, garbage out."

Keep garbage out of your mind. Empower yourself with positive thoughts and ideas.

Get rid of the trash.

Today.

Remember, being afraid to take tests is just a bad habit.

Your thoughts created the habit.

New thoughts can uncreate the habit.

TIME TO GO FOR IT

Are you just finishing a class or getting ready to graduate? Are you preparing to take your finals, your GED, college entrance exams, or driver's license?

Perhaps you are entering a new field of study and you feel your future depends on you passing some important test.

In the past (before you read this book) you probably would be exhausting yourself, staying up until the wee hours of the morning cramming, anxious, fearful, panicking about your ability to pass your test.

Not this time.

Instead you will learn new, proven ways to study. By listening to your MP3's every night you will prepare your subconscious mind for success.

You will choose to let no one or nothing stand in your way. You will choose to never let negative thoughts fill your mind. Just tell them to go away and find another game to play. You don't need them anymore.

You choose to be disciplined, motivated, and excited to do the work so you can achieve the success you desire and deserve.

Don't procrastinate. Start now.

Sense it.

Feel it.

Live it.

Do it.

How to Breathe

Another thing I'm going to teach you is how to breathe. Oh, I know you are breathing as you read this. But I want you to learn how to do deep breathing, the kind of breathing that oxygenates your brain so that you can think more clearly and relax as you begin to learn how to study. You always learn better when you are relaxed.

If you're like most people I work with, you probably do shallow, upper chest breathing as you study or take a test. Check yourself right now. Come on! Go ahead and take a deep breath and exhale. Do it now. That's right.

Did you lift your chest or shoulders up as you inhaled? Did you quickly blow out the air in your lungs as you exhaled?

Wrong! Wrong! Not very relaxing was it?

The proper way to do deep breathing is to relax your shoulders not lift up your chest at all. Instead you will inflate your belly as you inhale and suck it back towards your spine as you exhale.

Can't quite do it? Okay, it really is quite easy once you get the hang of it. Here's how you can learn to take those deep breaths. Get a letter size piece of paper – anything will do. Lie on your back on the floor or bed. Put a pillow beneath your head. Place the piece of paper on your belly. Inhale and lift the paper up by sticking out your belly as you breathe in. Then let the paper come back down as you open your mouth slightly and exhale as slowly as you can.

Come on. Try it again. Inhale, belly out. Exhale, belly in. See it's easy. You did it! Relaxing isn't it?

If you watch a baby sleeping, you will see they breathe this way naturally.

Inhale, belly out. Hold it. Open your mouth slightly and exhale very slowly, belly in.

For some of you this may be just the opposite of how you were taught to push your chest out and hold your belly in.

Do it right.

Practice makes perfect.

Deep breathe like this for three slow breaths in a row, three times a day.

C'mon, you can do it!

SECTION 2:
STUDYING FOR SUCCESS

CHAPTER 5:
YOUR STUDY SECRETS

BREATHE 7 – 11

You are now about to learn the secrets that will enable you to have very successful study habits. Once you get it, you'll be surprised to discover that you are now looking forward to studying. You are ready. No more procrastinating. Your work area is clean and organized.

When you sit down to study, sit up straight, close your eyes and take a deep relaxing breath. Inhale belly out. Open your mouth slightly. Exhale as slowly as you can.

As you do this think "7 – 11". Inhale to the count of 7 and exhale very slowly to the count of 11. This enables your brain to function at its highest capacity and in the most efficient way. Do three of these deep, relaxing breaths. Take your time.

Remember your magnificent brain weighs *only three pounds* but uses one third of all the oxygen you breathe in. Your brain needs oxygen to function and survive.

Quite often when you are in a room full of people taking tests you will hear people yawn or take deep sighs. They are not sleepy or frustrated; it's just the brain's way of getting oxygen so it can function better.

Therefore when you are studying, breathe as though your life depends on it.

Your studying does!

SAME PLACE

The next secret is so easy but so very important: As you begin your new way to study, always study in the same place. Whether you study in the library, or study hall, or at home, always study in the same place. By doing so, you will be instructing your powerful subconscious mind that it is now time to study.

Most often people study all over the place – in the kitchen, in the den, on the bed, at their desk, on the sofa while watching TV, in the car, at Starbucks. Is it any wonder that your subconscious mind doesn't get it that now is the time to breathe, relax, focus, and study?

However if you always study in the same place, your subconscious mind begins to associate the place you have chosen as the place where you study. It gets it. It begins to connect and understand, "Okay, now it's time for us to study. This is where we study." It is ready.

Studying in the same place over and over again will alert your subconscious mind that this is where and when you study. This simple action will enable you to begin to maximize your ability to focus and to retain what you study.

Your subconscious mind is your best friend.

It has incredible power. Use it!

SAME TIME

Your next secret of equal importance. If at all possible, always study at the same time. What we are doing is reprogramming your brain. No more procrastination, no more lack of discipline. Instead you choose the time to study, preferably the same time every day.

Be disciplined. Be committed and stick to it. Let nothing stand in your way.

You must select the time of day most suitable for you now, today. Early in the morning before breakfast? Before going to work or school? As soon as you come home, or after dinner? Choose the time that feels just right for you and then do it. Be committed to it. Have everything ready to get you started then go for it. Always give it all you've got.

Choose the length of time you will study. Remember, do it at the same time, in the same place on the days you have chosen – perhaps Monday through Friday and then take the weekends off. Or Monday, Wednesday, Friday, and Saturday while taking Tuesday, Thursday, and Sunday off. Whatever you choose, stick with it.

Don't get sidetracked. Just do it.

You are training your powerful subconscious mind to begin to work for you.

So use it.

Now.

Your future depends on it.

READ OUT LOUD

This next secret is *vitally* important.

You are doing great. You are getting it. Study in the same place. Study at the same time.

The next thing you'll learn is that whatever you are studying, reading, memorizing, read out loud!

That's right! You heard me! This is so incredibly important. You can read softly, but read out loud.

Now, get this next important part: Put your finger in one of your ears. Sound crazy? Well try it. Put your finger into one or both of your ears and say, "Hello Dr. Wanita." Do it!

Now take your finger out of your ear and say, "Hello Dr. Wanita."

Do it again.

Hear the difference?

Fun, isn't it?

With your finger in one or both of your ears it sounds like you have headphones on, then whatever you are reading goes deep into your subconscious mind. Even if you are almost silently mouthing the words, it slows you down. It sinks into your memory bank for you to be able to retrieve when you need it.

The reason that this is vitally important is that you are beginning to incorporate another sense into your studying. You are now using both visual and auditory. This will increase your retention of what you read, dramatically.

See the words.

Say the words.

Hear the words.

Learn the words.

TRACKING

Are you someone who gets to the bottom of the page and can't recall what you just read? Frustrating, isn't it? This indicates that you have trouble tracking from one sentence to the next, that often when you get to the end of a sentence you skip around and perhaps miss the next sentence, or reread the same one.

This happens so quickly in your brain that most often you are not even aware of it!

To help you not to do that, whether you are on a computer, Kindle, tablet, or a regular old-fashioned book, you will use a 3x5 card on the page you are reading. You will cover every sentence below the sentence you are reading and then move the card down just one sentence at a time.

This will slow you down and keep you focused on what you are reading. Of course if your screen or book is larger you can use a business-sized envelope.

Some of my clients have even cut a slit in the middle of the card or envelope so that only one sentence shows at a time. This really works to keep you totally focused only on what you are reading.

I promise you that by using this method of studying your material, you will remember what you have read and studied.

You are now using three of your senses in your studying. Visual (seeing), Auditory (hearing), and Kinesthetic (touch). This will enable you to absorb and retain all the information you are taking in.

You are now experiencing the joy of learning.

Practice seeing, hearing, and touching.

And...

Feel the magic beginning to happen.

TRICK YOUR MIND

By now you understand that you need to study in the same place at the same time; read out loud with your finger in your ear; use your 3x5 card; and take deep relaxing breaths. Remember, you always learn better when you are relaxed.

Always take three deep relaxing breaths before you start to study. Drop your shoulders down. Sit up straight. Relax. Get centered, quiet, focused. Get ready to study and trick your mind.

Before you begin you will need to have a timer that you can set for fifteen minutes. It can be any kind of timer – a kitchen timer, your mobile phone, your watch. Use whatever you have.

After a while you will be amazed that you will no longer need the timer. Your brain gets it and will automatically stop at fifteen minutes.

It has been discovered that the brain retains clearly what you study for the first fifteen minutes and what you study for the last fifteen minutes, with a big grey area in between.

So we are going to trick your brain by having you study in fifteen-minute increments. When fifteen minutes are up, STOP! Shake out your hands or do some jumping jacks. Get up and walk around a bit. Drink some water or juice (not alcohol). Stretch.

Then sit down again, sit up straight, and take three deep breaths to oxygenate your magnificent brain. Read out loud. Trick your brain and start another fifteen-minute session. You can study for 3-4 hours, but always in fifteen-minute segments with 60-seconds (or so) breaks in between.

You will be amazed at how much you retain by studying this way.

15 minutes – 4 hours – Breathe – Relax

Study as though your success depends on it.

It does.

FOCUSED, CENTERED, RELAXED

Okay, now that you have learned how to use your new study habits, you may discover you are really looking forward to studying. You are having very successful study periods and enjoying your new approach to studying.

You are completely focused when you study. You are enthusiastic and excited to learn. You are learning and retaining all that you need to remember. Everything begins to stick in your mind.

When you study, you concentrate. You shut out all sounds around you. You focus. You breathe. You remember.

You are getting it.

SECTION 3:
TESTING, TESTING: ONE, TWO, THREE

CHAPTER 6:
MOVE BEYOND FAILURE &
DREAM OF SUCCESS

TESTS, TESTS, MORE TESTS

How many tests do you think you have taken over your lifetime? Think. Go way back to your first grade spelling tests, penmanship tests, reading tests, arithmetic tests – tests that have gone on and on throughout your years.

It is mind-boggling when you stop to think about it. How many? It's impossible for you to count. So wouldn't you imagine after all these years, and all those tests, that the fear and anxiety connected with tests would have gone away? It doesn't.

I have worked for many years helping people learn how to take tests and I have discovered most people are terrified and paranoid about taking tests.

Where do you fit in? Do you get nervous and upset, and stay up night after night filling your mind with thoughts of failure? Do you wake up exhausted on the morning of your test? This is no way for you to start your test day and expect to be at your best.

In the previous chapters you have begun to affirm your self worth and you have learned and practiced your new rules for studying. These rules are very simple but very effective. You have practiced them and found that you have improved your memorization and your ability to retain information.

The next few chapters will teach you how to take your test; how to look forward to taking your test; how to reject failure and embrace success.

You will be ready!

Look forward to getting the results you want.

Tell yourself, "I will pass my test."

FANTASY OR REALITY?

Do you remember that your subconscious mind, the action part of your mind, doesn't know the difference between fantasy and reality?

Can I prove it?

Yes. I will, because I want you to get it.

Have you ever become frightened in a scary movie like Nightmare on Elm Street? Or held your breath as the Titanic was sinking? Or perhaps you've had a sexual fantasy? Are any of these things real? No! But your subconscious mind doesn't know the difference so it acts as if it is real.

Get it?

So why not fill your subconscious mind with wonderful, powerful thoughts about yourself and your test-taking abilities? Remember, it's your conscious mind that says "Yeah, but..." and it's your subconscious mind that does what it's told and acts as if it's real.

Do you get it that it's your mind that's the problem? Choose right now to step beyond failure and choose success. No longer fill your mind with fear of failure, negative stories, thoughtforms and labels that hold you back. These thoughts just get in the way and keep you from accepting all the powerful and positive qualities that you have.

Starting now, right now, this very moment – change! Fill your subconscious mind with new thoughts that will enhance your life. You don't even have to believe it at first. Just do it! Really do it.

You are what you think.

Remember – your conscious mind thinks the thought; your subconscious mind acts it out. Tell your subconscious mind good, powerful thoughts.

Get busy.

Get beyond failure.

Dare to dream success.

"F" Words

Starting now you agree not to use the "F" word. Ha! I know what you are thinking. No! I'm not talking about that "F" word!

I'm talking about Failure.

Get that "F" word out of your mind. Now! As long as you think you will fail, you will fail. When you tell your subconscious mind you will fail, it will produce toxic chemicals to prevent you from relaxing and recalling the information you have studied and stored in your subconscious mind.

Your recall system shuts down. You freeze up. You can't remember all the valuable information that would enable you to pass your test.

So no more "F" words.

No Failure.

No Fear.

No Frustration.

No Frenzy.

Let go of all your scary, negative thoughts. Let go of thoughts that weigh you down. Instead, beginning now, develop a powerful and positive mindset.

You have no use for those "F" words anymore. Give it up.

Keep going.

Study smart.

Discipline yourself.

Do the work.

Get on the road to success!

MANIFEST SUCCESS

Know that when it's time for you to take your test, you will be relaxed and ready. By now you have emptied your mind of all your fears. You have gotten rid of all the trash and all the old negative thoughts and stories. All the "F" words are now worthless and meaningless.

Conversely, you have now taken some giant steps. You have stepped outside the box. It wasn't always easy, but you did it. Now you value your worth. You are using your willingness to choose to refocus yourself and to reevaluate your potential.

You see, sense, and feel yourself as a winner. You are totally prepared to take your test. You have done the work. You have been disciplined. You have been committed. You have studied all that you need in order to pass your test and you have been listening to your MP3's every night.

Now prepare yourself even more.

But first a disclaimer! Be sure to check with your doctor before taking these or any other supplements!

Ten days before your test day, start taking zinc. Take the minimum dosage on the bottle. Zinc helps you think. Do this for just 10 days.

Also take vitamin E. Once again, only take the recommended minimum on the bottle. Vitamin E helps you oxygenate your blood and help you metabolize the oxygen. Your brain needs lots of oxygen in order to function at its highest level.

Also take calcium. It's Mother Nature's tranquilizer. Calcium will help keep you relaxed while taking your test. Take it for 10 days before your test.

This program will allow you to be relaxed, centered, focused. Continue to practice your deep breathing.

Now you know all you need to know to maximize your ability to pass your test.

And you will pass.

You are a winner.

CHAPTER 7:
TAKE THE TEST

GET READY TO GO FOR IT

To get the results you want, you made the decision to be committed to 21 days of doing the work. Studying, studying, studying, every day. Same place, same time. Reading out loud. Listening to your MP3's. Learning and practicing how to breathe. Working in fifteen-minutes of study time. Sitting up straight.

You've given it all you've got. You can do it!

It doesn't matter whether you are taking the LSAT, MCAT, College Entrance Exam, a grade school or high school mid-term or final exam, or even a driving test. It's all the same. What does matter is how you feel about yourself.

You choose to never again let testing upset or scare you. You can't think clearly when you're upset or scared. Instead tell yourself "I am prepared. I'm looking forward to finding out what I know or don't know."

Guess what? You know more than you think you know!

Having finished this book, having listened to your MP3's, and having used your new study habits all have enabled you to improve your memory and your ability to retrieve the information stored in your subconscious mind. This time you are very cool and relaxed about taking your test. You have overcome your weakness and improved your strength.

You have done the work.

Now...

Go for it!

Leonardo DiCaprio - Rewire Your Brain

In case you are wondering if your thoughts actually can change your brain and affect your ability to study and take tests, let me give you an interesting example:

When Leonardo DiCaprio was portraying Howard Hughes in the movie The Aviator, he called on Jeffrey M. Schwartz, M.D., an expert on neuroplasticity and OCD (obsessive-compulsive disorder) and the author of two brilliant books *Brain Lock* and *You Are Not Your Brain*. Hughes had suffered from OCD so DiCaprio asked Dr. Schwartz to help him understand how people with OCD think and behave.

DiCaprio didn't "act" like a person with OCD, but began thinking as a person with OCD and repeating those thoughts over and over. It began to change his brain. After a while, DiCaprio actually began to experience symptoms of OCD and it took him a while to get back to being himself.

This is called "neuroplasticity". We can change our brain with our thoughts, for better or for worse!

Thoughts create molecules. Molecules are measurable energy. Therefore you can create magic or chaos with your thoughts. Whether you think good thoughts or upsetting thoughts, depressing thoughts or empowering thoughts, your brain doesn't care.

Get it? Your brain always acts on your thoughts.

So now, as your test day approaches, affirm to yourself over and over:

"I have studied well."

"I am prepared to take my test."

I know all that I need to know to pass my test."

"I will rest my mind and my body two days before my test."

"I will pass."

21 Ways to Pass Your Test

1. Two days before your test, relax. Do not study.

2. Don't stay up late and exhaust yourself cramming.

3. On the morning of your exam you must eat. Not donuts, bagels, sweets, but protein – eggs, nuts, cottage cheese, etc. Your body and your brain need fuel. Also drink water.

4. If you are staying in a hotel, enjoy room service for your breakfast.

5. If you're not staying at a hotel, allow yourself plenty of time to get to your test area.

6. On your test day you will tell yourself, "I am relaxed, alert, clear-headed, relaxed." SMILE!

7. Dress warmly, in layers. Some test areas are very cold. It's impossible to relax if you are cold.

8. On your way to the test area, breathe. Fill yourself with oxygen. Your brain needs it.

9. Avoid having negative conversations with other test-takers.

10. Be a loner. Hold your own counsel.

11. Repeatedly affirm yourself as a winner.

12. When taking your test, sit up straight.

13. Breathe. Breathe. Breathe. Oxygenate that brain!

14. Take your time to think clearly.

15. Don't over explain essay questions. Answer only what is asked.

16. Always underline keywords as you write your answers to essay questions. This will help the person who grades your test know that you have addressed all of the main points.

17. If it's a multiple-choice question, know the answer is always there.

18. The most difficult questions are usually at the beginning. It's okay to skip them and go back later.

19. Answer questions that you know you know first. Then go back and answer questions that you are pretty sure you know.

20. If you have time, now answer the few remaining questions with an educated guess.

21. Answer simply, clearly, precisely and correctly.

Your best moment is always when what you don't know that you don't know becomes that which you now know that you do know.

Eureka! You are unstoppable now.

ATTENTION READER!

You must practice this last part of the book over and over again.

This is where you get to use your imagination. Every day, set aside some time to visualize yourself taking your test. Read the following pages to guide you in your visualization. Then close your eyes. Breathe. See it. Feel it. Sense it.

Continue doing this every day until there's no more tension, no more tightness, no more butterflies in your stomach. With repetition, all the old negative, frightening thoughts will be eradicated from your mind and your body.

Remember, as you think and feel, so shall you be. Do not be overly concerned about how this will work. Just do it. Have a deep conviction that through repetition it will work.

Focus on success.

Practice.

Practice.

Practice taking your test.

CHAPTER 8:
VISUALIZE YOURSELF ON TEST DAY

THIS IS IT!

Good morning!

Today is your day. You have had a good night's sleep. You are rested and ready.

You will have a light breakfast and drink plenty of water. You understand the importance of nourishing your brain and body.

You have put out your clothes the night before. It is time to get dressed and ready. You feel exhilarated, confident, and ready to go.

Whether you are walking, riding a bike, driving a car or a passenger on a bus, or on a train, empower yourself with positive thoughts. Tell yourself:

"I can do this."

"I know all that I need to know."

"I have done the work."

"My commitment in now paying off."

"My discipline is now paying off."

"My long hours of study are now paying off."

"I can handle this."

"I am satisfied with myself."

"I can hardly wait to get started."

Breathe, breathe, breathe.

Oxygenate your brain.

Get focused

TAKE THE TEST

See yourself entering the room where you will take your test. Feel and sense your energy. You have dispelled all negative beliefs about test-taking. You feel a tremendous feeling of positive power surging through you. You are filled with confidence.

You are very focused, centered, and grounded. You are so ready for this test. You are eager to get started. Only positive thoughts fill you now.

When you receive your test packet, you are excited and ready to begin. You can hardly wait to get started!

Picture it. Live it. Close your eyes and see, sense, and feel it.

You answer the questions quickly and correctly.

All of your work, all of your studying is now paying off.

Keep taking deep breaths; sit up straight; stay focused, centered, and grounded.

Enjoy yourself.

See, sense and feel yourself pass your test.

KEEP ON GOING

By now, nothing and no one can interfere with your ability to succeed. Not even you.

You are on a roll. You proceed quickly and calmly. You comprehend the questions and answer them correctly.

All of the information you have studied and stored in your subconscious mind is retrieved easily and effortlessly.

Remember to breathe big deep breaths. Give your brain the oxygen it needs to perform at its highest capacity.

If you don't know the answer to a question, no problem. Move on to the next question. Come back later and answer the questions you skipped. To your delight and surprise you probably will know the answers

Any questions left? Still have time? Now you can go back and take educated guesses on those questions.

Take your time. Relax. Enjoy.

You finish your test with time to spare.

You did it.

You are a winner.

You Did It

You did it! It's over! You finished with some time left over. You have been in the zone. You feel great. You know you passed. Your commitment and discipline have paid off.

All your selves – past, present, and future – were with you during your test, assuring you of your success. You are pleased with yourself. You feel secure about your test results. You answered most of the questions quickly and easily. You even surprised yourself about how much you knew to pass the test. All of your intelligence was with you as you took the test.

It is over. You feel wonderful. Gone are all the negative thoughts regarding test-taking. You now have the key. You know how to study like a pro. You get it. Studying in the right way is the answer. Relaxing and breathing while you study and while you take your test has helped make you a winner.

Now that your test is over you can continue to relax, unwind, and celebrate.

Let go and enjoy.

Be proud of yourself

You did it!

EASY TEST-TAKING FROM NOW ON

This book and your MP3's are filled with ordinary information that can and will produce extraordinary results. Your powerful new commitment has reeducated your subconscious mind and so doing has changed your attitude about test-taking and how to study forever.

So from now on, whenever any important test is approaching, get out this book and the companion *Stop Test Anxiety* MP3's and start reminding your subconscious mind (which has already been programmed) that you intend to be relaxed, and comfortable, and study well, and pass your next test.

No anxiety.

No "F" words.

Just positive reprogramming.

IT IS NOT MAGIC

Remember, to get the results you want, you have to do the work. You need to be disciplined and committed to doing the program. Did you fill your subconscious mind over and over again with the new thoughts that you needed to tell it? Or, did you continue to sabotage yourself by sending the wrong F word messages to your subconscious mind?

I am convinced that if you did the work faithfully as indicated in this book and that you did give it all you've got, that you will have ended your test anxiety. And only then, after you did the work, will it seem that magic has happened.

I promise that if you commit to doing this program and you listen to your MP3's for 21 days, you will experience empowering changes in the way you study and the way you approach test-taking. I am positive that these changes will take place if you simply do the work.

Remember to enjoy the process and be sure to let me know how this book and MP3's changed your life.

My Story

Twenty-seven years ago at the age of 57, I was out of work and down to $800 in the bank. I was living in a bedroom at a friend's house and desperately trying to figure out how I would survive. I was told I was too old for an entry-level job and too close to retirement for a corporate job. Desperate and depressed, I asked God, the Universe, Spirit Guides, Guardian Angels, or anyone who would listen, "What shall I do? What shall I do?"

I swear 'someone' kept whispering over and over again, "HYPNOTHERAPY!" I felt as though someone was just yanking my chain. Hypnotherapy? Again? No one is making a living doing hypnotherapy. But the whisper was very insistent and soon I could no longer ignore it.

To quiet the nagging in my mind, I got out the yellow pages (yes, there were yellow pages in those days!) and to my surprise I discovered there was actually a hypnotherapy school. Feeling a little foolish but determined to quiet the nagging voice in my head, I called the school. A delightful lady answered the phone and agreed to send me the school's information packet. When it arrived, I looked at it and thought, *New Age, airy-fairy stuff, make a living doing this? I don't think so.* And I threw it unopened into the trash.

Two weeks later the lady from the school called and asked me if I had read the material. I lied! I said it never came.

"That's odd," she said.

"Isn't it?" I replied.

"Let me check and see if I have the right address."

Of course she did. She then agreed to send me another packet. This time I opened it. The first thing I saw was that it required $500 to start the course. Once again, I tossed the packet into the trash. After all, I only had $800 to my name.

Once again, the lady from the school called. She said a lady had cancelled her reservation and would I be interested in taking that available space? I heard myself say yes. I wondered who said that? Where did that come from? I had a feeling that someone, something was guiding me, moving me on to my new life journey.

Desperation often makes you crazy, or courageous. So before I could change my mind, I wrote the check for $500, stuffed it in an envelope and raced to the post office. I wanted to put it in the outgoing mail before I could change my mind.

For about 24 hours, I was euphoric, filled with excitement. It did not last. Instead, I was now filled with fear, panic, and dread due to my impulsive behavior. "What the hell have I done?" I thought.

"Am I crazy? I need to get that money back! I will just go there and ask for a refund."

Driving down to the school, I became even more panicked. The freeway was crowded so I began to practice out loud what I would say when I got to the school. I made up dozens of excuses and why they should give me my money back. When I arrived, everyone was busy and it seemed inappropriate for me to ask for my money back at that time. So I decided that I would wait until the morning break and then go to the administration office to plead my case.

Two hours later I knew, whoever or whatever had pushed or guided me to this class knew better than I did. I never asked for my money back. That day I knew I had found my calling. It has been 27 years and I still have a full time hypnotherapy practice. Over the years I've worked with celebrities, politicians, rock stars, children, musicians, artists, students, writers, people from every walk of life, for every problem you could imagine. I have loved every moment of it.

I also have my own hypnotherapy school where I have trained hundreds of new hypnotherapists. I work very closely with my students. Because of my age, I long to pass on to my students all that I have learned over these many years. I tell my students, "My clients have taught me everything I know, and I'm going to teach it all to you."

Over the years I have been written up in *Elle, Cosmopolitan, Eve, Marie Claire, The London Herald, The Los Angeles Times, Larchmont Chronicle, The Santa Monica Evening Outlook,* and even *The National Enquirer!*

I've appeared on TV's *Good Morning London,* the BBC, *The Kilroy Show* (London), KABC *Early Morning* talk show, Regis Philbin's radio talk show, and many guest-speaking engagements.

My success came at an age when most people are ready to give up or retire. Remember, it is never too late to start over.

"Dr. Wanita is an inspiration to everyone she meets. She is a credit to her profession. Her love of life, her laughter and generosity of spirit, integrity, energy, and her indomitable spirit about never giving up, brings out the best in everyone she comes in contact with. She is a true Renaissance Woman!" ~ Aura Imbarus, author and speaker.

The "F" word... Again

Here it is: the "F word" again, only this time I want your Feedback!

Email, snail mail, voicemail, text, review on Amazon.com, whatever!

Tell me about your experience and your results from your new way of studying and taking tests. What worked for you? What seemed hard for you? Tell me what happened when you took your first test. What was your outcome? I will appreciate your feedback and I do look forward to receiving it. Make my day!

Also, let me know if I can use your comments on my website or any future books I'll be writing.

I do check my email daily. drwanita@gmail.com

To find out about my forthcoming books or to indicate a subject that you are interested in, contact me on my website: holmeshypnotherapy.com

Acknowledgments

To my family, friends, and my clients, who all
encourage me.

Thank you all.

You know who you are.

TESTIMONIALS

Dear Wanita,

You are truly a great friend. I find myself frequently thinking of you and sending you my positive thoughts AND I draw on your words of wisdom and encouragement in many ways. I want to thank you from the bottom of my heart for giving that boost I needed to get through the thickest time of my undergraduate career. You were my inspiration and I'm thrilled to share some wonderful news with you.

I have been accepted to Creighton University's School of Medicine!!! I got in!!! Yayyyyyy!!!!!

It was my first interview and first acceptance with 6 more schools pending as of right now so I will keep you posted.

I can't thank you enough for all your kindness and always believing in me. I hope our paths cross again soon.

Warm wishes,

Ariel M.
Santa Monica, California

Dear Dr. Wanita,

Thank you for teaching me how to study and how to take my LSAT. Remember how scared I was when I first came to see you? I passed the first time and was accepted to Law School in Florida. I could never thank you enough.

Bruce M.
Westwood, California

Dr. Wanita,

I passed my acupuncture exam! You inspired me to try again. I followed all your suggestions and listened to your cd. When it came time to place the needles, my hands were steady and I knew exactly where the points were. I could not have done it without your help. I especially thank you for all your encouragement and belief in me.

Sarah L.
Brentwood, California

"The Committee of Bar Examiners of the State Bar of California is delighted to report that you achieved a passing score on the February 1996 administration of the California Bar Examination. Congratulations; you may justly be proud of your achievement."

Thank you Dr. Wanita!

Julie Lee C.
Santa Monica, California

Wanita,

Thank you so much for helping me with my Science Fair project. I got an A!! You have been so much help to me. I couldn't have done it without you. I listen to your tapes whenever I feel the need to. It helps me clear everything negative from my head. I use the tools that you've taught me every day. You have done wonders for me and I just want to say thank you, so "Thank You."

I have more confidence in myself and I know I'm a good person. I love you.

Tim H. (age 10)
Los Angeles, California

I worked with Dr. Holmes for two visits and listened to my recording for three weeks. I passed my Bar Exam after having failed four times. I am so grateful to Dr. Holmes and could not have done it without her.

Michael K.
Torrance, California

Dear Wanita,

Edam has improved tremendously. He is getting off to school on time, he got all S's on his progress report from school and he seems altogether a happier person. There is always room for improvement of course, and there are still things he needs to work on - just like all of us have. It's a comfort knowing you are there when he needs you.

Thank you so much for everything.

All our love,
Sue M.
Los Angeles, California

Dear Wanita,

I just wanted to say thank you for all that you've done: for your work, your patience and understanding, and your encouragement, and your positive attitude and influence!! You have a wonderfully kind heart and smiling spirit. Thanks for sharing that through your work.

Leona T.
Los Angeles, California

NOTES

Made in United States
Troutdale, OR
10/12/2023

13640083R00072